PAPER & PEN = RELEASE

PAPER & PEN = RELEASE:

Poetic Prayers For The Weary Soul

Angel M. Atkins

Scribal House Publishing

Copyright © 2023, by Angel M. Atkins

All rights reserved.

Paper & Pen = Release: Poetic Prayers For The Weary Soul by Angel M. Atkins

Published by Scribal House Publishing, Chicago, IL 60652

Edited by Write With Heart, LLC, Charlotte, NC 28278

All rights reserved solely by the author. The author guarantees all contents are original and do not infringe upon the legal rights of any other person or work. No part of this publication may be reproduced, stored in a retrieval system or transmitted in any form by any means of electronic, mechanical, photocopying, recording or otherwise without the permission of the author.

ISBN-13: 979-8-9886497-0-0

Scripture quotations marked (KJV) are taken from the King James Version. All rights reserved.

Scripture quotations marked (ESV) are taken from the English Standard Version. All rights reserved.

Scripture quotations marked (NIV) are taken from the New International Version. All rights reserved.

Scripture quotations marked (NLT) are taken from the New Living Translation. All rights reserved.

Printed in the United States of America.

Contents

Introduction	1
Abandoned Wastelands	3
Approval Crawlers	7
Defeated Prism	11
Delay Tactics	15
Dungeon of Insecurity	19
My Name Sake	23
Peaceful Anxiety	27
Pride Zone	31
Rejected Chronicles	35
Shameful Places	39
Soul Cry	44
Timely Essence	48
Unrealistic Fantasies	52
War of Distractions Wonderland Cries	61
About The Author	65
Other Books by Angel M. Atkins	66

INTRODUCTION

When I wrote, **"Your Stop Is Here! 16 Truths That Will Move You From Fear to Faith,"** I received several heartfelt messages about the prayer in the book's introduction. I was emotional after hearing one reader's powerful testimony about their personal struggles. After reading the prayer, they felt the anointing and peace of God, which allowed them to release their burdens to Him. This moved me, prompting me to write **"Paper & Pen = Release: Poetic Prayers For The Weary Soul."** But, God led me down a different path. This prayer book is quite different from other books I've written. I initially set out to write a "regular prayer book" but I felt such a strong pull from the Holy Spirit to write these prayers poetically. It was essential for me to be fully authentic and vulnerable with my readers, which is a struggle for many, myself included.

While writing these prayers, I didn't hold back. Sometimes, I suppress my feelings with God out of fear He'll be angry with me. I'm a recovering perfectionist, so I'm sure you understand my point. Bearing this in mind, I decided to unashamedly tell God how I felt. If I was feeling afraid, tired, angry, worried, depressed, sad, happy, content, or optimistic, I revealed it all in **"Paper & Pen = Release: Poetic Prayers For The Weary Soul."** I was tired of suppressing my emotions. I wanted to be real with God without the mindset of what I thought He was expecting me to say. Oftentimes, I felt ashamed for having real life emotional experiences if I thought it wasn't in alignment with the will of God and I began to feel suffocated. So, my goal was to tell God everything that was on my heart. I need to be spiritually cleansed. The more I wrote, I realized I began to feel a little more comforted and a little lighter. My breathing became lighter and I began to experience peace. I suppose I was wrong for suppressing my feelings all along, right? It appears when I truly released everything to Him, only then did I experience this peace.

I believe this is also God's desire for *you*. He wants you to receive the peace your heart truly desires as you sincerely and authentically pour out your heart to Him. Similar to myself, many people hold back from their true feelings and expressions with God out of fear, but I believe this is the complete opposite of what God truly desires, which is for us to be real with Him. God wants our authenticity, not a robotic machine who repeats the same prayers day in and day out. Even though He knows exactly what we need and our desires, He patiently waits for us to come to the throne of grace and pour out to Him.

Today, I pray that you will make a decision to receive your spiritual cleanse by telling the Father about the things that are weighing down your heart. My prayer is as you read through each prayer, you, too, will see my passion and love for the Father in a raw and authentic way. My passion is not to give up despite life's difficulties, to preserve when people are against you, to love when it's most difficult, and to forgive and ask for forgiveness. Ultimately, my passion is to believe and follow Jesus Christ in my life. I believe you may be able to relate in some way. I pray that **"Paper & Pen = Release: Poetic Prayers For The Weary Soul"** will urge you to start pouring out NOW! I believe He is waiting to hear from you.

ABANDONED WASTELANDS

Father,

Thank You for a heart of sincerity.

Help me to consistently trust in You.

Never leave or forsake me like the people in my life do.

Selah.

My heart aches from the spirit of abandonment.

These wounds have left scars.

Rejection, loneliness, and desertion have taken a great toll on me.

I fear people will leave me.

I don't want to live like this.

I've been afraid to let go of the people that are not good for me.

I've become overly dependent on them.

I've allowed them to take advantage of me.

Heal my wounds from my past that still taunt me.

Heal wounds that are connected to my parents and

help me surrender thoughts of not being good enough

or loved by them.

Help me forgive those who have misused me.

Forgive me for the people I have mishandled out of fear.

Help me release these burdens to You.

They are too heavy to hold. I yield it all to You.

I place my life back in Your hands.

I believe I am safe.

Spirit of abandonment you have no control over me.

I'm no longer a victim because I live victoriously and

I'm sanctified by the Blood of Jesus Christ.

In Jesus' Name,

Amen.

Psalms 34:18 (ESV)

The LORD is near to the brokenhearted

and saves the crushed in spirit.

ABANDONED WASTELAND REFLECTION

1. What emotions did you experience while reading **ABANDONED WASTELANDS**?

   _____
   _____
   _____
   _____
   _____
   _____
   _____
   _____
   _____
   _____

2. Why do you believe these specific emotions occurred?

   _____
   _____
   _____
   _____
   _____
   _____
   _____
   _____
   _____
   _____

3. What is God saying to you?

_____
_____
_____
_____
_____
_____
_____
_____
_____
_____

4. What changes do you need to make?

_____
_____
_____
_____
_____
_____
_____
_____
_____
_____
_____

APPROVAL CRAWLERS

Father,

Thank You for loving and blessing me freely.

Thank You for Your love that is not based upon appearance only.

Thank you for Your amazing Grace and Mercy

that I could never earn.

Despite this truth

I've craved the world's

validation and truth.

I am guilty.

Forgive me.

I've desired praises of men over Your praise.

Desperately, I've wanted these worldly things.

My life has been full of stress and emptiness.

My standards have been lowered in different ways.

I've rejected Your truth.

You have always approved of me.

How could I ever forget?

I've allowed the enemy to trap me with distractions.

I've been consumed with the world.

Pressured to live a performance-based life.

But, this is all a lie.

Teach me Your precepts.

Break every chain connected with the spirit of darkness.

Separate me quickly and instantly.

Discernment is what I need.

Help me to remember who I am.

Free in Jesus, indeed.

No other approval

or validation is needed.

In Jesus' Name,

Amen.

Psalms 118:6-9 (ESV)

6 The Lord is on my side; I will not fear.

What can man do to me?

7 The Lord is on my side as my helper;

I shall look in triumph on those who hate me.

8 It is better to take refuge in the Lord

than to trust in man.

9 It is better to take refuge in the Lord than to trust in princes.

APPROVAL CRAWLERS REFLECTION

1. What emotions did you experience while reading **APPROVAL CRAWLERS?**

   _____
   _____
   _____
   _____
   _____
   _____
   _____
   _____
   _____
   _____

2. Why do you believe these specific emotions occurred?

   _____
   _____
   _____
   _____
   _____
   _____
   _____
   _____
   _____
   _____

3. What is God saying to you?

___

4. What changes do you need to make?

___

DEFEATED PRISM

Father,

Thank You for the good plans You have for me.

Your desire for my life is to be

full of good health and prosperity.

I know this is Your will.

At times, life is strenuous.

I feel like giving up and not wanting to live.

Life has taken a toil on me.

I can no longer bear it.

I feel defeated but I know *this* life isn't Your will for me.

Only good blessings come from You.

So, *this* can't be You.

Help me to remember today — my identity is in Jesus Christ.

Reveal the areas that have me locked in chains.

I renounce the negativity that I've spoken over my own life.

Father,

help my unbelief.

Only greatness lives on the inside of me.

Help me believe and receive Your truth.

I have real power to tread on serpents and scorpions.

Nothing shall hurt me.

I am no longer bound to the spirit of defeat.

I am an overcomer.

I am valuable and blessed.

Help me remember as a man thinketh, so is he.

I thank You for loving me.

I am free to be who You created me to be.

A new creature in Your eyes.

All things made new.

I am victorious in all things.

Your grace is sufficient.

Help me begin

again.

In Jesus' Name,

Amen.

Proverbs 23:7 (KJV)

For as he thinketh in his heart, so is he:
Eat and drink, saith he to thee; but his heart is not with thee.

DEFEATED PRISM REFLECTION

1. What emotions did you experience while reading **DEFEATED PRISM**?

   _____
   _____
   _____
   _____
   _____
   _____
   _____
   _____
   _____
   _____

2. Why do you believe these specific emotions occurred?

   _____
   _____
   _____
   _____
   _____
   _____
   _____
   _____

3. What is God saying to you?

　　_____
　　_____
　　_____
　　_____
　　_____
　　_____
　　_____
　　_____
　　_____
　　_____

4. What changes do you need to make?

　　_____
　　_____
　　_____
　　_____
　　_____
　　_____
　　_____
　　_____
　　_____
　　_____

DELAY TACTICS

Father,

Thank You that every blessing is for my highest good.

Everything is always done orderly and strategically,

even when I cannot see.

You are always producing things that are

life changing and life giving.

Thank You for orchestrating Your perfect timing in my life.

I've landed in the company of procrastination.

I've taken my life for granted.

I have deceived myself into believing

time never runs out.

Forgive me.

I've lost control

over things you have entrusted to me.

Help me make wise decisions and choices that will affect me

and those connected to me.

Help me to operate in the right mindset.

Remove anything that is causing delay.

Obedient is what I aspire to be.

I choose Your way,

Your strength,

Your wisdom.

I want to be

free.

In Jesus' Name,

Amen.

Proverbs 13:4 (NIV)

A sluggard's appetite is never filled,

but the desires of the diligent are fully satisfied.

DELAY TACTICS REFLECTION

1. What emotions did you experience while reading **DELAY TACTICS**?

   _____
   _____
   _____
   _____
   _____
   _____
   _____
   _____
   _____
   _____

2. Why do you believe these specific emotions occurred?

   _____
   _____
   _____
   _____
   _____
   _____
   _____
   _____
   _____

3. What is God saying to you?

   _____
   _____
   _____
   _____
   _____
   _____
   _____
   _____
   _____

4. What changes do you need to make?

   _____
   _____
   _____
   _____
   _____
   _____
   _____
   _____
   _____

DUNGEON OF INSECURITY

Father,

As a lost sheep, You sought me out

when I didn't know I needed to be found.

With the ultimate sacrifice of your son, Jesus Christ,

You paid for me.

I'm officially no longer condemned but forgiven.

I still need You more than I can comprehend.

Only You know the amount of pain and suffering I have endured.

I've been so insecure.

I'm taunted daily.

I'm always reminded that I am not good enough.

Low self-esteem has taken hold of me.

But I know these are lies sent

to kill, steal, and destroy.

You have come to bless me abundantly.

I need a great understanding of the truth.

I'm struggling with my identity,

which can only be found in Jesus Christ.

I need help rejecting these lies.

Seal all the pathways, airways,

and cracks at the entrance.

The enemy has entered illegally.

Perversion is what I see.

Lies have caused my life to be dark and full of torment.

Replace these lies with Your light of truth.

Heal wounds from my childhood.

Break every generational curse of insecurity.

My life will be lived whole to declare the works of the Lord.

Turn my mourning into fullness of joy.

Your plan for me is only for prosperity.

I am

free.

In Jesus' Name,

Amen.

John 10:10 (NLT)

The thief's purpose is to steal and kill and destroy.

My purpose is to give them a rich and satisfying life.

DUNGEON OF INSECURITY REFLECTION

1. What emotions did you experience while reading **DUNGEON OF INSECURITY**?

   _____
   _____
   _____
   _____
   _____
   _____
   _____
   _____
   _____
   _____

2. Why do you believe these specific emotions occurred?

   _____
   _____
   _____
   _____
   _____
   _____
   _____
   _____
   _____
   _____

3. What is God saying to you?

_____
_____
_____
_____
_____
_____
_____
_____
_____
_____

4. What changes do you need to make?

_____
_____
_____
_____
_____
_____
_____
_____
_____
_____

MY NAME SAKE

I contemplate death often

as if

it's calling my name.

Then, I hear

echos of fear

taunting me

and doubt

questioning my beliefs.

Yet,

I still have hope.

Father, forgive me.

Sometimes,

I feel invincible

when I don't fall for the lies.

But,

days feel longer when I don't believe.

Days, lengthen me please.

I won't go out like this,

I've suffered too much.

Lead me along the path

for Your name's sake.

Show me a better way.

Open my heart.

I need the truth.

Whose voice will I listen to?

It has to be

You.

Psalm 31:3 (KJV)

For thou art my rock and my fortress;

therefore for thy name's sake lead me, and guide me.

MY NAME SAKE REFLECTION

1. What emotions did you experience while reading **MY NAME SAKE**?

   _____
   _____
   _____
   _____
   _____
   _____
   _____
   _____

2. Why do you believe these specific emotions occurred?

   _____
   _____
   _____
   _____
   _____
   _____
   _____
   _____

3. What is God saying to you?

_____
_____
_____
_____
_____
_____
_____
_____
_____
_____

4. What changes do you need to make?

_____
_____
_____
_____
_____
_____
_____
_____
_____
_____

PEACEFUL ANXIETY

Father,

You know exactly how I feel and

the words I'm about to say.

Yet,

You still listen to me.

You know I'm in need of Your peace.

I've allowed anxiety to take over many areas of my life.

My days have become heavy with worry, fear, and dread.

I am constantly in mental turmoil,

which leads to depression and fear.

Help me, today, to release these cares to You.

I've taken on too much in my life,

worrying about things I cannot control.

Help me not to conform to a world that only brings death.

Help me to believe.

Fill these anxious areas with your peace and comfort.

Calm my anxious mind.

Deliver me from anxiety.

I receive Your peace today.

In Jesus' Name,

Amen.

2 Thessalonians 3:16 (KJV)

Now the Lord of peace himself

give you peace always by all means.

The Lord be with you all.

PEACEFUL ANXIETY REFLECTION

1. What emotions did you experience while reading **PEACEFUL ANXIETY**?

   _____
   _____
   _____
   _____
   _____
   _____
   _____
   _____
   _____
   _____

2. Why do you believe these specific emotions occurred?

   _____
   _____
   _____
   _____
   _____
   _____
   _____
   _____
   _____
   _____

3. What is God saying to you?

_____
_____
_____
_____
_____
_____
_____
_____
_____
_____

4. What changes do you need to make?

_____
_____
_____
_____
_____
_____
_____
_____
_____
_____

PRIDE ZONE

Father,

Thank You for the blessing and privilege

to boldly come to the throne of Grace.

Thank You for always hearing my prayers and

for always being patient with me.

Thank You for helping me,

especially

when life seems the hardest.

I've been struggling.

The spirit of pride

has caused me to stumble and trip.

It has caused me to lose friends, family, and opportunities.

I've been arrogant and overconfident in areas I shouldn't have been.

I've lived in deception, rejecting help when it's most needed.

Forgive me.

Selah.

This is not the life You want for me

Root out this spirit of pride that only wants to confuse and mislead.

Fill my heart with humbleness and humility.

I cannot do it on my own.

Help me grab hold of this truth.

Remind me that I am nothing without You.

Real strength is only found in You.

I'm no longer partaking in this worldly thing.

I choose to thrive with You in this life.

My expectations are in You.

Holy Spirit, help me to do what is right.

Father, powerfully shine Your Glory in my life.

In Jesus' Name,

Amen

Proverbs 16:18 (KJV)

Pride goeth before destruction,

and an haughty spirit before a fall.

PRIDE ZONE REFLECTION

1. What emotions did you experience while reading **PRIDE ZONE**?

   _____
   _____
   _____
   _____
   _____
   _____
   _____
   _____
   _____
   _____

2. Why do you believe these specific emotions occurred?

   _____
   _____
   _____
   _____
   _____
   _____
   _____
   _____
   _____
   _____

3. What is God saying to you?

   _____
   _____
   _____
   _____
   _____
   _____
   _____
   _____
   _____

4. What changes do you need to make?

   _____
   _____
   _____
   _____
   _____
   _____
   _____
   _____
   _____

REJECTED CHRONICLES

Father,

Thank You for Your love that never fails,

Your attentiveness that never forsakes me and

for never growing tired of me.

I've allowed some things to take root in my life recently.

Rejection is her name.

I've suffered endless days and nights.

A life full of anger, hatred, jealousy, and sorrow.

My days are broken, burdened, and tormented —

too much to name.

Please forgive me for allowing this.

I know this is not the life You desire for me.

I've become tired and restless.

Peace, I need now.

Reveal Your love for me deeply.

Move powerfully in my life,

so that there will be no residue.

Uproot the lies of shame,

not being good enough,

and unworthiness.

Break the strongholds and generational curses.

Lead me by the power of the Holy Spirit.

Redeem my soul.

Make me new.

Transfer me into the Kingdom of light

where there is all truth.

Fill my heart with pure love and joy.

Allow my feet to reach the path destined for me.

Heal me.

In Jesus' Name,

Amen.

Jeremiah 30:17 (ESV)

For I will restore health to you,

and your wounds I will heal,

declares the LORD,

because they have called you an outcast:

'It is Zion, for whom no one cares!'

REJECTED CHRONICLES REFLECTION

1. What emotions did you experience while reading **REJECTED CHRONICLES**?

   _____
   _____
   _____
   _____
   _____
   _____
   _____
   _____
   _____
   _____

2. Why do you believe these specific emotions occurred?

   _____
   _____
   _____
   _____
   _____
   _____
   _____
   _____

3. What is God saying to you?

   _____
   _____
   _____
   _____
   _____
   _____
   _____
   _____
   _____

4. What changes do you need to make?

   _____
   _____
   _____
   _____
   _____
   _____
   _____
   _____
   _____

SHAMEFUL PLACES

Father,

I've experienced a lot of difficulties in my life

but Your word still proves true.

You have not forsaken me.

You have been here for me through it all.

Thank You.

With You,

I can be transparent,

offering honesty and humility.

I have endured so much in my life —

loss, disappointment, and guilt.

But, the spirit of shame has caused the greatest damage.

Fear of embarrassment and judgment,

caused reluctancy

to admit my faults.

I've been in denial,

I've felt undeserving of the things You have placed in my heart.

I've felt unworthy of your love and blessings.

My self-esteem has been stripped.

The thought of earning everything has disrupted my life.

I've accepted things beneath me,
struggling desperately.

Only You know how this spirit has tried to control me.

Feeling trapped,

peace is not within me.

My life doesn't reflect the abundant life You died to give me.

I will not call You a liar.

Deliver me today.

Open my heart that I may receive Your powerful truth for my life.

I am worthy, loved, and no longer seen by You as guilty

Open my heart and

allow me to receive Your truth — I am a victor and no longer guilty.

Help my unbelief.

As I confess sin to you, thank You for your forgiveness.

I am accepted and loved by You.

Condemnation has been nailed to the cross with Jesus Christ.

I am no longer condemned or found guilty.

Magnify Your word in my life

Transform *me*.

In Jesus' Name,

Amen.

Isaiah 61:7 (ESV)

Instead of your shame there shall be a double portion;

instead of dishonor they shall rejoice in their lot;

therefore in their land they shall possess a double portion;

they shall have everlasting joy.

SHAMEFUL PLACES REFLECTION

1. What emotions did you experience while reading **SHAMEFUL PLACES**?

   _____
   _____
   _____
   _____
   _____
   _____
   _____
   _____
   _____
   _____

2. Why do you believe these specific emotions occurred?

   _____
   _____
   _____
   _____
   _____
   _____
   _____
   _____
   _____
   _____

3. What is God saying to you?

   _____
   _____
   _____
   _____
   _____
   _____
   _____
   _____

4. What changes do you need to make?

   _____
   _____
   _____
   _____
   _____
   _____
   _____
   _____

SOUL CRY

Father,

The truth is that

I've believed the enemy's lies.

He told me he loved me.

I gave him all of me.

He left me feeling unworthy.

His eyes glistened upon my places and

he covered me with his kisses.

But I was left

empty.

No love was between us.

Where is the love?

I looked above.

Someone please answer me.

Do You ever hear me?

Hello…?

Where is the voice from Heaven?

The clouds surround me.

A formed heart in the sky.

Could it be true?

My heart's cry has reached the Holy places.

He lied to me.

You always heard me.

In Jesus' Name,

Amen.

Psalm 91:15 (ESV)

When he calls to me, I will answer him;

I will be with him in trouble;

I will rescue him and honor him.

SOUL CRY REFLECTION

1. What emotions did you experience while reading **SOUL CRY**?

   _____
   _____
   _____
   _____
   _____
   _____
   _____
   _____
   _____

2. Why do you believe these specific emotions occurred?

   _____
   _____
   _____
   _____
   _____
   _____
   _____
   _____
   _____

3. What is God saying to you?

   _____
   _____
   _____
   _____
   _____
   _____
   _____
   _____
   _____
   _____

4. What changes do you need to make?

   _____
   _____
   _____
   _____
   _____
   _____
   _____
   _____
   _____
   _____

TIMELY ESSENCE

Breathe in.

Breathe out.

We are in

the land of the living

but one day,

it will not be so.

How will you show up today?

His glory awaits us.

Surrender —

give up now.

Don't hold back.

We are *too* blessed.

Guide my days into Your greatness, Father.

Silence sounds below.

Allow my voice to reach You now.

Open my heart to Your voice.

Let me see

who You've made me to be.

Forgive me.

You've waited long enough.

I get it.

Fill me up.

Revive me.

Refine me.

The

time

is

now.

Isaiah 38:18-19 (NIV)

18 For the grave cannot praise you,

death cannot sing your praise;

those who go down to the pit

cannot hope for your faithfulness.

19 The living, the living—they praise you,

as I am doing today;

parents tell their children about your faithfulness.

TIMELY ESSENCE REFLECTION

1. What emotions did you experience while reading **TIMELY ESSENCE**?

   _____
   _____
   _____
   _____
   _____
   _____
   _____
   _____
   _____
   _____

2. Why do you believe these specific emotions occurred?

   _____
   _____
   _____
   _____
   _____
   _____
   _____
   _____
   _____
   _____

3. What is God saying to you?

   _____
   _____
   _____
   _____
   _____
   _____
   _____
   _____
   _____

4. What changes do you need to make?

   _____
   _____
   _____
   _____
   _____
   _____
   _____
   _____
   _____

UNREALISTIC FANTASIES

Father,

my mind wanders off to a place

where there's only You and me.

Now, I get it.

Some who deliver Your message

give me a newsy vibe,

which is not my preference.

Their energy is aggressive

when they sit and speak.

But, people like me,

we walk and talk energetically.

Now, I see.

It all makes sense.

I wondered if I didn't appreciate

their version of truth due to their demeanor.

But when I heard them speak,

I saw the truth.

Peace.

They don't fit the criteria.

Who am I to say such a thing?

My criteria?

But, it's true.

My distinctiveness is unique.

I have a spiritual connection to those like me.

I just want to be me.

They have shamed and ridiculed us.

They laugh and say we're doing too much.

I see our likes are different.

We've become problems and liars to some

because our energy is too much.

Who is my spirit drawn to?

Where are you?

I didn't see this until now.

Energy and connection are vital.

Perhaps I've forgotten these truths.

Thank You, Father,

for loving

me.

In Jesus' Name,

Amen.

Psalm 139:14 (KJV)

I will praise thee; for I am fearfully and wonderfully made: marvellous are thy works.

UNREALISTIC FANTASIES REFLECTION

1. What emotions did you experience while reading **UNREALISTIC FANTASIES?**

_____
_____
_____
_____
_____
_____
_____
_____
_____
_____

2. Why do you believe these specific emotions occurred?

_____
_____
_____
_____
_____
_____
_____
_____
_____
_____

3. What is God saying to you?

_____
_____
_____
_____
_____
_____
_____
_____
_____
_____

4. What changes do you need to make?

_____
_____
_____
_____
_____
_____
_____
_____
_____
_____

WAR OF DISTRACTIONS

Father,

Thank You for life.

Your words are the light of my life that brings complete fullness.

Your ways are perfect.

Forgive me for drifting

into the world of distractions.

I haven't focused on the things above.

My actions are not a reflection of the Kingdom.

I've been following in the enemy's footsteps,

along his pathway

of darkness that's been laid out for me.

Slippery.

I cling to the world's way,

doing more to get done faster

but this has only caused a great delay.

I need to focus on what is needed.

Please forgive me.

I know this spirit is here to confuse me.

Father, help me

reject the lies of deception and hindrances.

Help me with consistency.

Help me to be effective and work efficiently.

Redeem the time.

Resurrect me.

Your light and revelation allows me to be free.

Realign my steps and renew my mindset.

All things are possible with You.

Holy Spirit, lead and guide me.

Father, bless me.

Peace, You leave with me.

In Jesus' Name,

Amen

1 Peter 5:8 (ESV)

Be sober-minded; be watchful.

Your adversary the devil prowls around

like a roaring lion,

seeking someone to devour.

WAR OF DISTRACTIONS REFLECTION

1. What emotions did you experience while reading **WAR OF DISTRACTIONS?**

   _____
   _____
   _____
   _____
   _____
   _____
   _____
   _____
   _____
   _____

2. Why do you believe these specific emotions occurred?

   _____
   _____
   _____
   _____
   _____
   _____
   _____
   _____
   _____
   _____

3. What is God saying to you?

_____
_____
_____
_____
_____
_____
_____
_____
_____
_____

4. What changes do you need to make?

_____
_____
_____
_____
_____
_____
_____
_____
_____
_____

WONDERLAND CRIES

Father,

love me with the type of love I've only read about.

I dream of the day my heart absorbs Your

love fully.

Gaze upon me with Your glory.

Love me in my mess.

Make me spotless.

Clean me up

until I sparkle.

This is a dream —

the need

to be perfect

but perfection doesn't exist.

Only Your love gets me.

Heal me,

fulfill me,

and honor me, Father.

Love me tender.

Is this the way?

Draw me into Your undeserving love for me.

Tell me.

Only Your voice matters.

Fill me up.

Replenish me.

Revive me.

Make me whole.

Now, I know the

truth.

In Jesus' Name,

Amen.

> ***John 8:32 (NIV)***
> *Then you will know the truth,*
> *and the truth will set you free.*

WONDERLAND CRIES REFLECTION

1. What emotions did you experience while reading **WONDERLAND CRIES?**

   _____
   _____
   _____
   _____
   _____
   _____
   _____
   _____
   _____
   _____

2. Why do you believe these specific emotions occurred?

   _____
   _____
   _____
   _____
   _____
   _____
   _____
   _____
   _____
   _____

3. What is God saying to you?

_____
_____
_____
_____
_____
_____
_____
_____
_____
_____

4. What changes do you need to make?

_____
_____
_____
_____
_____
_____
_____
_____
_____
_____

ABOUT THE AUTHOR

Angel M. Atkins is a wife, girl mom of three, publisher of Scribal House Publishing, writer, author, and speaker. She is highly anointed, best known for her prophetic boldness. Her greatest desire — and life purpose — is to encourage, motivate, and influence people to live more fulfilling and impactful lives in the Kingdom of God. She believes God has already provided the blueprint for people to live a successful life by utilizing their gifts and talents for God's Glory. She is passionate about exposing light and truth where there has been darkness, igniting purpose, dreams, and vision. She is committed to helping people regain the focus and determination needed to be all God has called them to be.

OTHER BOOKS BY ANGEL M. ATKINS (ANGEL M. WALKER)

YOUR STOP IS HERE!

16 TRUTHS THAT WILL MOVE YOU FROM FEAR TO FAITH

RAINDROPS OF INSPIRATION

INTIMATE CONFESSIONS

BETWEEN YOU & ME (Blank Journal)

JUST WRITE (Blank Journal)

Books are available on Amazon.com*

www.ingramcontent.com/pod-product-compliance
Lightning Source LLC
Chambersburg PA
CBHW070103100426
42743CB00012B/2644